Santa Barbara

A concise and Detailed Itinerary Handbook to a
Memorable Adventure, Discovery and Insider's
Experiences

SANTA BARBARA

Travel Guide

2024

Elis Tello Rios

BONUS:

- Itineraries
- Insider's Tips
- Family Vacation
- Solo Travelers Tips
- Romantic Adventure
- Delectable Images
- Detailed Maps
- Restaurant & Shopping
Guide

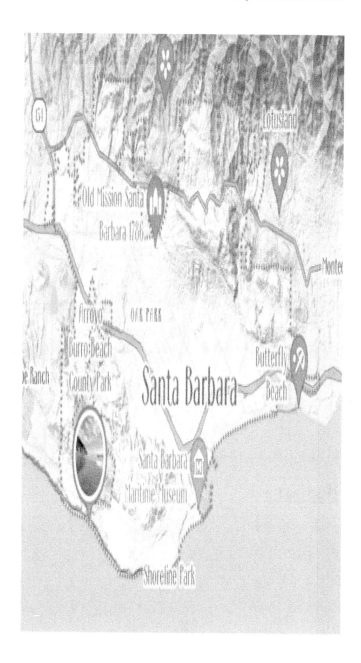

Scan QR With Device to Navigate Around **Santa Barbara**

Disclaimer

This publication, " Travel Guide 2024," is provided for Experience & informational purposes only. The authors and publishers have made every effort to ensure the accuracy and reliability of the information provided within this book. However, the information is presented "as is" without warranty of any kind.

The author do not accept any responsibility or liability for the accuracy, content, completeness, legality, or reliability of the information contained in this guide. No warranties, promises, and/or representations of any kind, expressed or implied, are given as to the nature, standard, accuracy, or otherwise of the information provided in this publication nor to the suitability or otherwise of the information to your particular circumstances.

The information in this guide may be updated, amended, or changed at any time without notice. Therefore, we recommend verifying any critical information with local authorities, service providers, and/or legal advisors before making travel plans or decisions.

The authors and publishers shall not be liable for any loss or damage of any nature whatsoever, whether direct, indirect, consequential, or other, whether arising in contract, tort, or otherwise, which may arise as a result of reliance on the information contained in this book, or any other information provided in connection with it, including, but not limited to, changes in dates, times, prices, or other factual details.

Use of this guide implies acceptance of this disclaimer.

Extra Chapters

- Itineraries
- Insider's Tips
- Family Vacation
- Solo Travelers Tips
- Romantic Adventure
- Delectable Images
- Detailed Maps
- Restaurant & Shopping Guide

Bonus!

A B O U T   T H E   A U T H O R

Elis Tello Rios: A Connoisseur of Wanderlust

In the world of travel and exploration, Elis Tello Rios stands out as a distinguished author and authority. With a passion for discovering the hidden gems of every destination, Elis has dedicated her life to the art of travel. Her expertise is not just in traversing the globe but in capturing the essence of each place she visits, making her a revered travel guide expert.

Born to a family of avid travelers, Elis's journey began in her childhood, traversing diverse cultures and landscapes. Her fluency in several languages, including Spanish, English, and French, has enabled her to connect deeply with people and places around the world. Elis holds a degree in Anthropology, further enriching her understanding of different cultures and histories, which is evident in her detailed and insightful writing.

Her extensive travels have taken her to over 70 countries, each experience contributing to her vast knowledge and unique perspective on travel. Elis is not just a tourist but a true explorer at heart, seeking out not only the popular sights but also the off-the-beaten-path treasures.

Elis's writing style is engaging and informative, making her guides not just helpful tools for travelers but also enjoyable reads for anyone fascinated by the world. This "Travel Guide 2024" is a testament to her expertise, offering a comprehensive and captivating look at one of South Africa's most vibrant cities.

When she's not globe-trotting or penning her next guide, Elis enjoys sharing her experiences through lectures and travel blogs, inspiring others to embark on their own adventures. Her passion for travel is matched only by her commitment to providing travelers with the knowledge they need to have enriching and memorable journeys

What You Will Find Here......

INTRODUCTION

As soon as I step foot in the center of Santa Barbara, the city's unique combination of Spanish colonial history and contemporary Californian charm captivates me. The gorgeous shoreline of the city—fondly referred to as the American Riviera—unfolds before me, framed by undulating hills. Every street has its narrative to tell, full of colorful ethnic manifestations and a wealth of historical detail.

The whitewashed houses and red-tiled roofs that adorn the charming downtown streets enthrall me. I can smell the scent of freshly made food from the area, luring me in to enjoy delectable dishes that showcase the city's wide range of culinary preferences. The weather in Santa Barbara is as pleasant as its residents; a bright sky and a mild sea breeze provide for year-round bliss that promotes outdoor activities.

As I continue my exploration, I find myself attracted to the city's well-known historical sites, such as the Santa Barbara Mission, which bears witness to its long past. The city's creative fabric is enhanced by a plethora of artistic creations, ranging from sophisticated galleries to street murals.

Santa Barbara exhibits a distinct fusion of scenic splendor, cultural diversity, and a hospitable vibe at every turn.

I'm inviting you to explore this seaside jewel and all of its numerous gems by using this guide. Greetings from Santa Barbara, a place where every visitor may discover a little bit of heaven of their own.

History and Culture

California's coastal sanctuary of Santa Barbara is a tapestry woven with many cultures and rich history. The Chumash people, whose influence is still ingrained in the fabric of the city, called it home at first.

The remarkable Spanish colonial architecture of the city is evidence of the new period ushered in by the advent of Spanish explorers in the 16th century. The "Queen of Missions," the Mission Santa Barbara, is a symbol of this historical shift, providing insight into the early religious and cultural landscape of the city.

Layers of history reveal themselves to me as I walk about the El Presidio Historic Park, narrating tales of Spanish troops, Mexican control, and finally American colonization.

The city has been profoundly impacted by these ages, resulting in a distinct cultural mosaic. Every year, the city celebrates its rich history with several festivals and events. One such event is the Old Spanish Days Fiesta, which revives the city's past with traditional cuisine, dancing, and music.

As varied as Santa Barbara's past is, so too is its cultural landscape. Art and creativity flourish here, from the internationally renowned Santa Barbara Museum of Art to the quirky Funk Zone. The city is also known for its vibrant music culture, which attracts visitors and artists from all over the world with events like the Santa Barbara International Film Festival and the Santa Barbara Bowl performances.

Geographic Overview

Tucked away between the Pacific Ocean and the Santa Ynez Mountains, Santa Barbara has a breathtakingly varied topography. The city's coastline provides beachgoers and lovers of the ocean with a paradise of immaculate beaches and charming ports. A few of the highlights along this length include East Beach, which has volleyball courts and beautiful vistas, and Butterfly Beach, which is well-known for its breathtaking sunsets.

The city is dramatically framed by the lush paths and expansive views of the Santa Ynez Mountains. Every time I go on an excursion in the Santa Ynez Valley or go hiking in the Los Padres National Forest, I am struck by how beautiful the surrounding landscape is.

Renowned for producing some of California's best wines, the area is also known for its wine country, which is home to several vineyards and wineries.

The flora and wildlife of Santa Barbara are diverse due to its unique geographic location. The region's distinctive microclimate fosters a range of habitats, including oak woods and coastal wetlands, each of which is home to a unique kind of fauna. As the "Galapagos of North America," the neighboring Channel Islands National Park is proof of this abundant biodiversity.

Weather and Best Times to Go

Santa Barbara's weather is often characterized as Mediterranean, with warm, dry summers and moderate, rainy winters. The city is a great visit all year round because of the beautiful weather. The mid-60s to mid-70s Fahrenheit is the normal temperature range, which makes the weather perfect for outdoor activities and exploration.

In Santa Barbara, summertime is a flurry of activity. The city is busy with festivals and events, and the beaches come alive with surfers and sun worshippers. Whether you're sailing along the coast or climbing in the mountains, this is the ideal time of year to explore the great outdoors. But, guests should be prepared for the sporadic "June gloom," a maritime layer that appears in the morning and usually clears by the afternoon.

Santa Barbara has an extra allure in the fall because of the reduced number of people and better weather. As the grape harvest and autumn foliage form a stunning backdrop for wine tastings and vineyard excursions, this season is especially enchanting in wine country.

Winter is a great season for people to travel since it's still very warm and has plenty of sunlight, even if it's colder outside. Seasonal rains revitalize the environment and provide the city with a calm atmosphere that is ideal for romantic dinners and strolls along the beach.

In Santa Barbara, springtime is a celebration of rebirth. The pleasant weather is perfect for seeing the city's outdoor attractions and historic buildings, while the hillsides and gardens are bursting with brilliant hues.

Santa Barbara is a year-round destination for tourists looking for beauty, culture, and adventure since each season has something special to offer. Santa Barbara always has something unique in store, whether it's the soft caress of the spring air or the warm embrace of the summer sun.

Keeping Memories

Getting to Santa Barbara

Air Travel and Airports

Flying into Santa Barbara is a quick and beautiful way to get there. The Santa Barbara Airport (SBA), which serves the city, is a quaint and effective facility whose Spanish-style design perfectly reflects the essence of the area.

SBA, which is just ten miles west of the city center, has a variety of domestic flights that link Santa Barbara to important American destinations. Flying into SBA is a unique experience; as the jet descends, passengers are rewarded with breathtaking aerial views of the Santa Ynez Mountains and the shoreline.

The Los Angeles International Airport (LAX) is a good substitute for individuals who are traveling abroad or are looking for more airline possibilities. Situated around 100 miles to the southeast of Santa Barbara, LAX is a globally recognized airport with a vast network of both domestic and international flights. Travelers may use the Amtrak Pacific Surfliner rail or other modes of transportation, such as shuttle services, to get to Santa Barbara from LAX, or they can take a picturesque drive down the Pacific Coast Highway.

Road and Rail Connections

Road travel to Santa Barbara is every bit as charming as the actual destination. The city is conveniently accessible via U.S. Highway 101 follows the coast of California. The drive is a must-do activity while visiting Santa Barbara because of the amazing vistas of the surrounding scenery and the Pacific Ocean along this route. The roadway offers an easy and picturesque path right into the center of the city for those arriving from the north or south.

An option that is just as picturesque and soothing is rail travel. Santa Barbara is connected to locations around Southern California, such as San Diego, Los Angeles, and San Luis Obispo, via Amtrak's Pacific Surfliner service. Various scenic parts of the train ride along the coast provide unhindered views of the ocean and beaches. Situated among several activities and lodging options, the historic landmark Santa Barbara rail station is easily accessible from downtown.

Overview of Local Transportation

Once in Santa Barbara, traveling about is a snap because of the extensive and welcoming transit infrastructure in the city. With most of the main sights, eateries, and retail establishments conveniently located within walking distance, the downtown area is small and very walkable. The city provides a variety of transportation alternatives for individuals who want to go further in their exploration.

The Goleta, Carpinteria, and Montecito suburbs, as well as the city itself, are served by the extensive bus services offered by the Santa Barbara Metropolitan Transit District (MTD). The buses provide regular trips to well-known

locations and are an effective and reasonably priced means of getting throughout the city.

Scan QR to Navigate <u>**Santa Barbara Gardens**</u>

The Santa Barbara Trolley Company provides guided tours of the city, offering a pleasant overview of the main attractions and history, for a distinctive local experience. This hop-on, hop-off service is ideal for those who want to see the city's top attractions at their leisure.

Another common form of transportation is cycling, which is encouraged by the city's many bike trails and bike-friendly streets. For example, the lovely waterfront path of the Cabrillo Bike Path is perfect for taking in the city's breathtaking scenery.

Finally, a plethora of taxis and ride-sharing services are accessible for your convenience, making it simple to go from one area of interest to another at any time of day or night.

In Santa Barbara, traveling by car offers a distinct viewpoint of this beautiful seaside city, making the trip as delightful as the destination.

Keeping Memories

Accommodations

Luxury Hotels

Santa Barbara, a city known for its beauty and splendor, is home to some of California's best hotels. The Four Seasons Resort The Biltmore Santa Barbara, situated at 1260 Channel Drive, is a prime example.

This legendary hotel offers visitors an amazing experience as it lies magnificently by the seaside, fusing contemporary luxury with Spanish colonial history. Every element of this place exudes luxury, from the verdant grounds to the private beachside entrance. Due to its popularity, reservations may be made over the phone or online, with rooms sometimes reserved months in advance.

The Belmond El Encanto, located at 800 Alvarado Place and tucked away in the hills, is another jewel. With its expansive views of the city and the Pacific, this hotel is a peaceful refuge. Travelers with high standards love the Belmond El Encanto because of its fine meals and customized service.

Its infinity pool and spa treatments add to its charm, making it the ideal getaway for anybody looking to unwind in an opulent environment.

It's best to make reservations well in advance, particularly during busy times.

Mid-Range Options

Several mid-range lodging options in Santa Barbara guarantee a great stay for people looking for comfort without the high cost. Situated in the center of downtown at 533 State Street, the Hotel Santa Barbara is distinguished by its excellent location and quaint atmosphere.

With its unique combination of contemporary conveniences and historical elegance, this historic hotel places visitors in the center of the thriving arts and culture of the city. Making reservations is simple and may be done over the phone with the hotel.

The 28 W Cabrillo Boulevard Harbor View Inn is another great midrange option.

This hotel, which has a view of the lovely Santa Barbara Harbor, combines luxury and convenience. It is the perfect place for both business and family tourists, with features including an on-site spa and pool as well as convenient proximity to the beach and Stearns Wharf. It is advised to make reservations in advance, particularly during summer and holiday weekends.

Budget and Hostel Stays

In Santa Barbara, there are several possibilities for vacationers on a tight budget. Situated in the Funk Zone at 12 E Montecito Street, The Wayfarer is a hip hostel that provides shared dorm beds as well as individual rooms. It's a terrific place for single travelers and young explorers wishing to meet other travelers, and it's well-known for its lively environment and public areas. Online bookings are available, and it's best to make them in advance, particularly during the busiest travel times.

The IHSP Santa Barbara, located at 111 N Milpas Street, is a dependable option for those on a limited budget. There are private and shared room choices available at this hostel, which offers simple, tidy lodging. It's a convenient starting point for seeing the city since it's close to beaches and well-known sites. Reservations may be made online, and early booking is advised due to its reasonable price.

Unique Local Stays

Additionally, Santa Barbara offers distinctive lodging options that provide a more distinctive and regional experience. Encircled by beautiful English gardens, the Victorian estate that is the Simpson House Inn, a bed and breakfast, is situated at 121 E Arrellaga Street. It provides excellent service, beautifully furnished rooms, and a calm, private atmosphere. For those looking for a tranquil escape or a romantic weekend, this hidden treasure is ideal. Reservations must be made in advance, either over the phone or online.

The Autocamp Santa Barbara, located at 2717 De La Vina Street, is another unique choice. This little Airstream motel puts a distinctive spin on conventional travel accommodations. Stylish furnishings and contemporary conveniences are included in the specially constructed Airstream trailers that host guests.

For those who want to try something new, it's an elegant and daring option. It's best to make reservations in advance since this unique lodging gets booked up fast.

Keeping Memories

Dining and Cuisine

Fine Dining Restaurants

A gastronomic journey, Santa Barbara's fine dining scene offers a fusion of nuanced tastes and outstanding dining experiences. The Lark, at 131 Anacapa Street, is a highlight.

Reputably known for its artisanal approach, this restaurant offers visually stunning and delectably gorgeous farm-to-table food. The Central Coast's tastes influence the seasonal variations in the cuisine. It is advised to make reservations, which may be done over the phone or online.

Bouchon, located at 9 W Victoria Street, is another outstanding restaurant. This little eatery serves French-inspired food made using ingredients that are obtained locally.

Bouchon is a haven for wine connoisseurs and wine aficionados alike, with an extensive wine selection that features the best of Santa Barbara. It's best to make reservations in advance, particularly for weekend eating.

Casual and Street Food

There are several informal and street food alternatives available in Santa Barbara for a more relaxed eating experience. A neighborhood favorite is La Super-Rica Taqueria, located at 622 N Milpas Street. Renowned for its genuine Mexican cuisine, this modest restaurant rose to prominence with Julia Child's support. There will be a queue, but the waiting will be worth it for their famous tacos and tamales.

Foodies should not miss the Santa Barbara Public Market, which is situated at 38 W Victoria Street. A variety of vendors selling anything from wood-fired pizzas to gourmet ice cream can be found at this busy market. It's the ideal place to have a leisurely meal and take in the cuisine of the area.

Cafés and Bakeries

The café culture of Santa Barbara is lively and varied. Handlebar Coffee Roasters is distinguished by its great coffee and friendly environment. It has two locations: 128 E Canon Perdido Street and 2720 De La Vina Street. This neighborhood roastery is a terrific place to get freshly baked pastries and a cup of gourmet coffee.

Jeannine's Restaurant & Bakery, at 1253 Coast Village Road, is another well-liked location. Jeannine's, well-known for its delectable breakfast and brunch fare, also offers a selection of baked pastries that are guaranteed to please any sweet craving. Enjoying your dinner in a pleasant location is possible with their outside seats.

Local Delicacies and Food Tours

It is essential to sample the local fare in Santa Barbara if you want to truly immerse yourself in the culinary scene. Here, seafood is a mainstay, with uni (sea urchin) and Santa Barbara spot prawns among the delicacies. With a view of the water and some of the freshest seafood, Brophy Bros. is located at 119 Water Way.

Guiding culinary excursions are available via Santa Barbara Food excursions for people who want to sample a range of regional delicacies.

These excursions take you to several areas where you may sample cuisine from different restaurants and discover the history and culture of the city's culinary scene. These excursions are a great way to discover the variety of Santa Barbara's food options, and reservations may be made online.

Dining in Santa Barbara is an enjoyment as much as a means of subsistence. The city's culinary scene, which offers everything from elegant restaurants to informal nibbles, is a tribute to its rich cultural past and abundant local vegetables. Whatever your level of culinary expertise, Santa Barbara's eating scene is sure to please your palette and enhance your vacation.

Keeping Memories

Santa Barbara Activities and Attractions

Historical Sites

The historical landmarks of Santa Barbara provide witness to the city's illustrious past. A must-see is the Mission Santa Barbara, which is situated at 2201 Laguna Street.

This 18th-century site, dubbed the "Queen of the Missions" for its breathtaking beauty, provides an insight into the history of California's missions. There are guided tours that give you an understanding of its historical importance and architecture.

El Presidio de Santa Barbara State Historic Park, located at 123 E Canon Perdido Street, is another important historical landmark. This historic military post, which dates to 1782, was significant to the history of Santa Barbara. Explore the renovated structures and displays that highlight the history of Spanish colonization in the city.

Galleries and Museums

One of Santa Barbara's cultural highlights is the Museum of Art, which is situated at 1130 State Street. It provides a varied artistic experience with a collection that encompasses both contemporary and historical pieces. The museum is well-known among art enthusiasts for its displays of European, Asian, and American art.

The Museum of Contemporary Art Santa Barbara, located at 653 Paseo Nuevo, is a fascinating place for fans of contemporary art. This location offers a distinctive viewpoint on contemporary artistic trends by showcasing cutting-edge works by regional, national, and international artists.

Nature Reserves and Parks

The Santa Barbara Botanic Garden, 1212 Mission Canyon Road, will appeal to nature lovers. This 78-acre park has tranquil strolling routes across a variety of environments and is devoted to native flora found in California. It's the ideal location for a leisurely walk and to take in the breathtaking scenery of the area.

Extending outside the municipal boundaries, the Los Padres National Forest provides a wide wilderness region ideal for trekking, camping,  and animal observation. Enjoying beautiful pathways and expansive vistas, it's a sanctuary for nature lovers looking to go back to nature.

There are many different things to do and see in Santa Barbara, from peaceful gardens to daring wildlife reserves, from historical landmarks to contemporary art galleries. Every site provides a distinctive experience that reflects the natural and cultural diversity of the city. In the captivating setting of Santa Barbara, visitors may enjoy the great outdoors, engage with art, or learn about history.

Keeping Memories

Shopping and Local Crafts

Shopping Districts

Santa Barbara's retail areas are as varied as they are lovely, providing everything from high end boutiques to quirky local stores. State Street, the city's main avenue, is a thriving retail center. Lined with a variety of businesses, from well-known retail giants to smaller boutiques, State Street caters to a range of preferences and budgets. The region is also home to several restaurants and cafés, making it perfect for a full day of shopping and eating.

Another noteworthy retail district is the Funk Zone, along the waterfront. Shopping in this area is more cutting-edge because of its unique blend of stores, restaurants, and art galleries. It's a terrific spot to discover unique goods and get involved with the neighborhood's artistic community.

Local Markets

The Santa Barbara Certified Farmers Market is a must-visit if you want a taste of local culture. This market, which has many venues around the city on various days, is an exhibition of the area's abundant agricultural produce. Fresh fruit, handmade items, and gourmet delicacies are available for purchase here. Additionally, it's a fantastic chance to network with nearby farmers and producers.

Another feature is the Santa Barbara Artisan Market, which takes place every Sunday at 236 E Cabrillo Blvd. Handcrafted goods made by regional artists are available at this outdoor market, including textiles, ceramics, and jewelry. It's the ideal location to discover one-of-a-kind, handcrafted gifts and souvenirs.

Souvenir and Specialty Shops

There are many of specialist stores in Santa Barbara for individuals looking to buy mementos. The charming retail center La Arcada, located at 1114 State Street, has a range of specialized shops selling anything from exquisite art to handcrafted chocolates. It's the perfect place to find excellent and distinctive mementos.

Another fantastic place to get mementos is The Santa Barbara Company, which is situated at 214 E Victoria Street. This store focuses on presents with a Santa Barbara theme and regional items including home goods, wines, and olive oils that are obtained locally. It's a terrific location to locate a keepsake that perfectly embodies Santa Barbara.

Santa Barbara's unique character and creative flare are reflected in the shopping experience itself. The city provides a range of shopping experiences that appeal to all tastes and give a real piece of the Santa Barbara experience to take home, from busy retail areas to charming local markets and from upscale shops to handcrafted crafts.

Keeping Memories

Festivals & Events in Santa Barbara

Cultural Festivals

Santa Barbara's creative vitality and diversified culture are vividly reflected in its cultural events. Renowned in the film industry, the Santa Barbara International Film Festival attracts both celebrities and movie buffs. This yearly festival includes panel discussions, prizes, and a wide range of films, from independent releases to global blockbusters.

The Old Spanish Days Fiesta, which honors the city's strong Spanish past, is another noteworthy cultural event. This August celebration includes parades, traditional flamenco dance, and a bazaar with regional cuisine and handicrafts. This vibrant and exciting festival perfectly embodies Santa Barbara's rich history.

Music and Art Events

For fans of music, the outdoor amphitheater known as the Santa Barbara Bowl presents a range of events with well-known performers from many genres. This location, which is well-known for its cozy atmosphere and breathtaking vistas, offers a remarkable musical experience outside beneath the stars.

Fans of the arts will enjoy the Santa Barbara Arts & Crafts Show, which has been held annually since 1965. Every Sunday, local artisans and artists set up shop along Cabrillo

Boulevard to showcase their creations, which include anything from handcrafted jewelry and pottery to paintings and photographs. It's a fantastic location to see and buy regional art.

Seasonal Events

Santa Barbara's calendar is enhanced with seasonal events. Bright floats, costumes, and performances highlight the amazing creative show of the June Santa Barbara Summer Solstice Parade. It's a beloved holiday for both residents and tourists, commemorating the longest day of the year.

The Santa Barbara Harbor and Seafood Festival honors the area's seafood sector every October throughout the winter. A flavor of the local marine culture is offered by this festival, which also includes boat trips, cookery demos, and fresh seafood.

The festivals and events of Santa Barbara provide an insight into the city's artistic, cultural, and seasonal customs. These events, which showcase the city's rich history and lively sense of community, provide engaging experiences via cinema, music, art, and seasonal festivals.

Keeping Memories

Useful Information

Safety and Health

In general, Santa Barbara is a secure and health-conscious location. Standard travel insurance should be carried by visitors to cover unforeseen medical requirements. Access to first-rate medical treatment is ensured by the city's many well-equipped clinics and hospitals, including the Santa Barbara Cottage Hospital at 400 W Pueblo Street.

It's always a good idea to be mindful of your surroundings, particularly in tourist-heavy locations, and to heed any health recommendations issued by the local government, especially those related to hiking trails and beach safety.

Currency and Banking

The US Dollar (USD) is the currency in use. While most places take credit cards, it's a good idea to have cash on hand for any minor transactions or in case your card is denied.

There are many of ATMs in the city, particularly in the areas with plenty of stores and close to popular tourist destinations. Banks and some hotels provide currency conversion services, although it's usually more cost-effective to do this ahead of time.

Communication and Connectivity

Santa Barbara has excellent access to mobile services and high-speed internet. Free WiFi is often offered in cafés, hotels, and some public spaces. When traveling abroad, it's a good idea to inquire about roaming fees with your service provider or, if you want to remain longer, think about getting a local SIM card.

For local calls, Santa Barbara's area code is 805; this information is helpful.

Local Customs and Etiquette

Santa Barbara is renowned for its amiable and carefree vibe. Most establishments allow casual clothes, however, certain exclusive clubs or restaurants may insist on more formal attire. In the US, tipping is expected; 15-20% is the going rate for excellent service in pubs and restaurants. Tipping hotel employees, cab drivers, and tour guides are also considered courteous.

Living sustainably is ingrained in the native way of life. Particularly at public parks and beaches, visitors are urged to respect nature by avoiding littering and by sticking to authorized routes. The city is also bike-friendly, with many residents choosing to pedal instead of drive, which is indicative of a broader inclination toward environmentally responsible behaviors.

Being aware of these practical factors will guarantee a relaxing and pleasurable stay in Santa Barbara, making it easy for tourists to fully immerse themselves in the way of life and culture of the area.

Day Trips and Excursions from Santa Barbara

Nearby Towns and Natural Wonders

Solvang: The distinctive Danish-style community of Solvang, which is just 45 minutes away from Santa Barbara, is well-known for its windmills, bakeries, and wines. The town's exquisite pastry shops and classic Danish architecture provide a taste of small-town Europe.

Los Olivos: A must-visit for wine connoisseurs, Los Olivos is renowned for its neighborhood wine-tasting establishments, art galleries, and boutique stores. This charming village perfectly captures the essence of California's wine valley.

Channel Islands National Park: These islands, which are reachable by boat from

Ventura, provide an excellent haven for those who like the outdoors. Hiking, kayaking, and animal viewing are among the available activities. The area has beautiful natural scenery and abundant marine life.

Ojai: Well-known for its calm atmosphere and creative community, Ojai is the ideal destination for anybody looking for a quiet getaway. Spa services, regional art galleries, and the breathtaking Ojai Valley landscape are available to visitors.

Carpinteria: Conveniently located near Santa Barbara, Carpinteria has stunning beaches, such as the well-known Carpinteria State Beach, renowned for its serene surf and picturesque surroundings.

Wine Country Tours

Santa Ynez Valley and Santa Rita Hills are two of the most well-known wine regions in the Santa Barbara region. Many tour operators provide  guided wine-tasting excursions, which give guests the chance to visit many vineyards, see how wine is made, and taste a range of regional wines. These excursions are a practical way to see the area's vineyards and sample some of the greatest Californian wines since they often include transportation.

Guided Tours and Activities

Activities and guided excursions abound for people who want to see more of the region. These may include culinary sampling excursions, historical city walks, and whale viewing excursions in addition to coastal kayaking experiences. Adventure seekers may take part in coastal sailing trips or horseback riding in the Santa Ynez Mountains.

It's simple to discover Santa Barbara's many attractions and scenic splendor since many firms provide excursions that may be customized to fit a variety of interests.

These day trips and excursions provide a sense of the wide range of experiences that Santa Barbara and the surrounding area have to offer, from the peace of tiny villages and natural reserves to the thrill of outdoor activities and the extravagance of wine country tours. They appeal to all interests.

Keeping Memories

Additional Chapters

Annual Calendar of Events in Santa Barbara

January

Santa Barbara International Film Festival: A celebration of cinematic art featuring international and independent films.

February

Santa Barbara Gourmet Dining Week: Showcasing the best of local cuisine with special menus and events.

March

Santa Barbara Orchid Show: One of the largest orchid shows in the United States.

April

Earth Day Festival: Environmental exhibits, workshops, and activities.

May

Santa Barbara Wine and Food Festival: Local wineries and chefs offer tastings and pairings.

June

Summer Solstice Parade: A vibrant celebration with costumes, floats, and music.

Santa Barbara French Festival: Celebrating French culture with food, music, and dance.

July

Fourth of July Fireworks and Festival: Fireworks show and family-friendly activities at the waterfront.

Santa Barbara Greek Festival: Traditional Greek food, music, and dance.

August: Fiesta Santa Barbara: A historic festival celebrating the city's Spanish heritage.

September: Santa Barbara Seafood Festival: Seafood tastings, cooking demonstrations, and ocean activities.

October

Santa Barbara Harbor and Seafood Festival: Fresh seafood, maritime education, and boat rides.

Santa Barbara Vintners Festival: Wine tastings from over 100 local wineries.

November: Santa Barbara International Marathon: A scenic marathon and half-marathon.

Dia de los Muertos Celebrations: Cultural festivities honoring the deceased.

December

Santa Barbara Parade of Lights: Boat parade and fireworks show.

Holiday Market: Local crafts, food, and holiday-themed events.

Helpful Phrases with Pronunciation Guide

Hello / Goodbye
"Hola / Adiós" (OH-lah / ah-dee-OHS)

Please / Thank you
"Por favor / Gracias" (por fah-VOHR / GRAH-see-ahs)

Yes / No
"Sí / No" (SEE / NO)

How much is this?
"¿Cuánto cuesta esto?" (KWAHN-toh KWEHS-tah EHS-toh)

Where is...?
"¿Dónde está...?" (DOHN-deh EHS-tah)

I would like...
"Me gustaría..." (meh goos-tah-REE-ah)

I need help
"Necesito   ayuda"   (neh-seh-SEE-toh
ah-YOO-dah)

Do you speak English?
"¿Habla inglés?" (AH-blah een-GLAYS)

I don't understand
"No entiendo" (noh ehn-TYEHN-doh)

Can I get the bill?
"¿Me trae la cuenta?" (meh TRAH-eh lah
KWEHN-tah)

I'm allergic to...
"Soy alérgico/a a..." (soy ah-LEHR-hee-koh/ah
ah)

Where is the bathroom?
"¿Dónde está el baño?" (DOHN-deh EHS-tah el BAH-nyoh)

Excuse me
"Disculpe" (dees-KOOL-peh)

I'm lost
"Estoy   perdido/a"   (ehs-TOY pehr-DEE-doh/dah)

What time is it?
"¿Qué hora es?" (keh OH-rah ehs)

Can you help me?
"¿Puede   ayudarme?"   (PWEH-deh ah-yoo-DAR-meh)

I'm looking for...
"Busco..." (BOOS-koh)

Cheers! (when toasting)
"¡Salud!" (sah-LOOD)

Good morning / Good night
"Buenos días / Buenas noches" (BWEH-nos DEE-ahs / BWEH-nahs NOH-chehs)

Enjoy your meal
"Buen provecho" (bwen proh-VEH-choh)

These phrases, along with their pronunciations, will be helpful for English-speaking tourists navigating Santa Barbara and interacting with locals.

Keeping Memories

Sample Itineraries

Family-friendly Adventure:
Day 1: Visit the Santa Barbara Zoo and spend the afternoon at East Beach.
Day 2: Explore the Santa Barbara Museum of Natural History and enjoy a picnic at Alameda Park.

Solo Travelers:
Day 1: Wander through the Santa Barbara Botanic Garden and explore the Funk Zone for art and dining.
Day 2: Join a group hike in the Santa Ynez Mountains and enjoy a wine tasting tour.

Romantic Adventure:

Day 1: Stroll through the Santa Barbara Rose Garden, followed by a sunset cruise.

Day 2: Relax at a spa and dine at a fine restaurant overlooking the ocean.

Culinary Adventure:

Day 1: Visit the Santa Barbara Public Market and join a cooking class.

Day 2: Go on a food tasting tour in the city, followed by a visit to local wineries.

These appendices enrich the travel guide, providing practical information and suggestions to help visitors plan their trip and experience the best of Santa Barbara throughout the year.

Santa Barbara Restaurant Guide with Local Recipes

Santa Barbara's culinary scene is a vibrant mix of local flavors and global influences. This guide features a selection of restaurants along with descriptions of local dishes and recipes, giving visitors a taste of the region's gastronomic delights.

The Lark - Artisanal California Cuisine

Location: Funk Zone
Must-Try Dish: Santa Barbara Sea Urchin
Recipe Highlight: Local Sea Urchin Crostini - Fresh sea urchin served on toasted crostini with lemon zest and a drizzle of olive oil.
Tip: Reserve in advance and ask for a seat on the patio for the best experience.

Loquita - Authentic Spanish Tapas

Location: State Street

Must-Try Dish: Paella Mixta

Recipe Highlight: Traditional Paella Mixta - A mix of seafood, chicken, and chorizo, cooked with saffron-infused rice and vegetables.

Tip: Great for sharing; pair with a Spanish red wine.

Santa Barbara Shellfish Company - Seafood Specialties

Location: Stearns Wharf

Must-Try Dish: Local Spiny Lobster

Recipe Highlight: Spiny Lobster Tacos - Grilled lobster meat served in a soft taco shell with fresh salsa and lime.

Tip: Visit during lobster season (October to March) for the freshest catch.

Bouchon - Wine Country Cuisine

Location: Downtown

Must-Try Dish: Wine-Braised Short Ribs

Recipe Highlight: Wine-Braised Short Ribs - Slow-cooked short ribs in a rich wine sauce, served with seasonal vegetables.

Tip: Ask for wine pairing recommendations from their extensive local selection.

Mesa Verde - Plant-Based Delights

Location: Mesa

Must-Try Dish: Stuffed Avocado

Recipe Highlight: Quinoa-Stuffed Avocado - Ripe avocado halves filled with seasoned quinoa, topped with pico de gallo and cashew cream.

Tip: Perfect for a light lunch; their outdoor seating is ideal on sunny days.

Brophy Bros. - Harborfront Seafood

Location: Harbor

Must-Try Dish: Clam Chowder

Recipe Highlight: Creamy Clam Chowder - A rich blend of clams, potatoes, and cream, seasoned with fresh herbs.

Tip: Enjoy the chowder with a view of the boats; arrive early to beat the crowds.

This guide, with its blend of restaurant recommendations and local recipes, offers a comprehensive look at Santa Barbara's dining scene. Visitors can indulge in these culinary experiences, or even try their hand at creating some of these dishes to relive their Santa Barbara memories at home.

Keeping Memories

Santa Barbara Shopping Guide for Visitors

Santa Barbara offers a delightful shopping experience, from chic boutiques and local markets to distinctive shopping districts. Here's a guide to the best shopping spots in the city, complete with insider tips.

State Street & Downtown Area

Location: State Street, Downtown Santa Barbara

Hours: Generally 10 AM - 8 PM

Description: This bustling area is the heart of Santa Barbara shopping, with a mix of well-known brands, unique local shops, and art galleries.

Popular Items: Designer clothing, handcrafted jewelry, art pieces.

Insider Tip: Check out the local boutiques tucked away in the side streets for one-of-a-kind items.

The Funk Zone

Location: Between State Street and Garden Street

Hours: Varies by store, typically 11 AM - 7 PM

Description: A hip, artsy neighborhood known for its eclectic mix of artisan shops, galleries, and wine tasting rooms.

Popular Items: Local artworks, handmade crafts, boutique wines.

Insider Tip: Many shops here are small independent businesses, so you'll find unique items not available elsewhere.

Santa Barbara Public Market

Location: 38 W Victoria Street

Hours: 7 AM - 11 PM

Description: An indoor marketplace offering a variety of local goods, from gourmet foods to artisan products.

Popular Items: Specialty foods, local olive oils, handmade soaps.

Insider Tip: Perfect for picking up picnic supplies or unique Santa Barbara souvenirs.

La Arcada Plaza

Location: 1114 State Street

Hours: 10 AM - 6 PM

Description: A charming, picturesque plaza with a selection of boutiques, galleries, and dining options.

Popular Items: Fine art, luxury clothing, unique gifts.

Insider Tip: Visit during the evening for a beautiful, ambient shopping experience.

Montecito's Lower Village

Location: Coast Village Road, Montecito

Hours: 10 AM - 5 PM

Description: An upscale area known for its luxury boutiques and high-end shops.

Popular Items: Designer apparel, luxury home decor, fine jewelry.

Insider Tip: The area is known for its high-end goods, so be prepared for premium pricing.

Santa Barbara Arts and Crafts Show

Location: Cabrillo Blvd., East of Stearns Wharf

Hours: Sundays, 10 AM - 6 PM

Description: An outdoor market showcasing the works of local artisans and craftsmen.

Popular Items: Handcrafted jewelry, paintings, photography.

Insider Tip: Great place to meet the artists and negotiate prices on original pieces.

Each of these destinations offers a unique shopping experience, reflecting the diverse character of Santa Barbara. Whether you're looking for luxury items, local crafts, or just a leisurely shopping stroll, these places have something for every visitor. Remember to check the opening hours before you go, as they can vary, especially on holidays.

Keeping Memories

Made in the USA
Las Vegas, NV
14 January 2024

84323125R00046